1 MONTH OF
FREE
READING

at

www.ForgottenBooks.com

By purchasing this book you are eligible for one month membership to ForgottenBooks.com, giving you unlimited access to our entire collection of over 1,000,000 titles via our web site and mobile apps.

To claim your free month visit:
www.forgottenbooks.com/free1118541

ISBN 978-0-331-40010-6
PIBN 11118541

This book is a reproduction of an important historical work. Forgotten Books uses
state-of-the-art technology to digitally reconstruct the work, preserving the original format
whilst repairing imperfections present in the aged copy. In rare cases, an imperfection in
the original, such as a blemish or missing page, may be replicated in our edition. We do,
however, repair the vast majority of imperfections successfully; any imperfections that
remain are intentionally left to preserve the state of such historical works.

FOR RELEASE
JULY 8, P. M.
1954

The
LIVESTOCK and MEAT
SITUATION

LMS-72

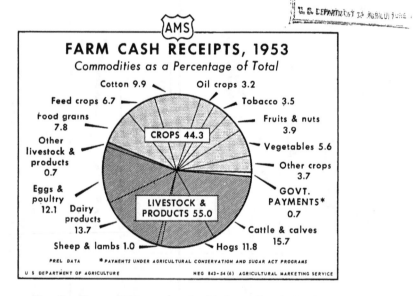

FARM CASH RECEIPTS, 1953
Commodities as a Percentage of Total

Cotton 9.9 — Oil crops 3.2
Feed crops 6.7 — Tobacco 3.5
Food grains 7.8 — Fruits & nuts 3.9
Other livestock & products 0.7 — Vegetables 5.6
CROPS 44.3 — Other crops 3.7
Eggs & poultry 12.1 — GOVT. PAYMENTS* 0.7
Dairy products 13.7 — LIVESTOCK & PRODUCTS 55.0 — Cattle & calves 15.7
Sheep & lambs 1.0 — Hogs 11.8

PREL DATA   *PAYMENTS UNDER AGRICULTURAL CONSERVATION AND SUGAR ACT PROGRAMS
U S DEPARTMENT OF AGRICULTURE   NEG 843-54 (6) AGRICULTURAL MARKETING SERVICE

More than 28 percent of farmers' cash receipts last year came from meat animals. Meat animals, dairy and poultry products combined made up 55 percent of the total.

Receipts from cattle and calves have been the largest single source of income since 1945, when they superseded dairy products as the leader.

UNITED STATES DEPARTMENT OF AGRICULTURE
AGRICULTURAL MARKETING SERVICE

2

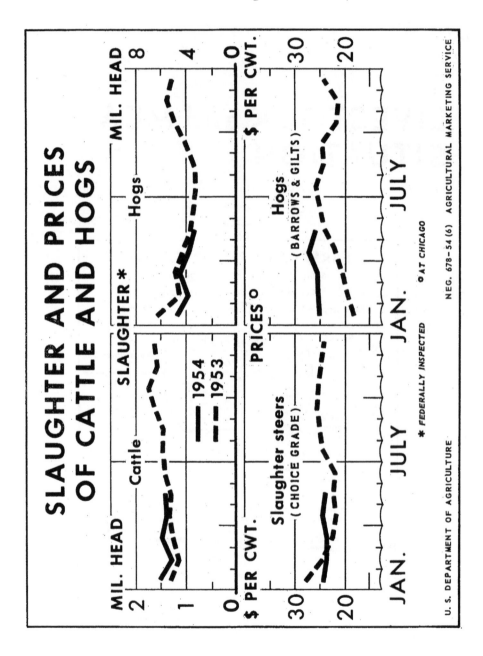

SLAUGHTER AND PRICES OF CATTLE AND HOGS

U. S. DEPARTMENT OF AGRICULTURE

NEG. 678-54 (6)   AGRICULTURAL MARKETING SERVICE

* FEDERALLY INSPECTED   ○ AT CHICAGO

T H E ·L·I·V E S T O C K A N D M F A T S I T U A T I O N

Approved by the Outlook and Situation Board, June 30, 1954

SUMMARY

        The livestock situation will be featured this summer and fall by
a substantial increase in the number of hogs slaughtered, reflecting more
spring pigs saved than last year, and by cattle slaughter at about the
same high volume as in the last half of 1953. Slaughter of sheep and
lambs may be a little below the same period last year. Total output of
red meat will be somewhat over a year ago.

        Prices received by farmers for cattle and calves are likely to
average generally about the same as last year. Prices for hogs will be
moderately lower.

        The 1954 spring pig crop was 13 percent larger than the 1953 crop.
Also, farmers reported on June 1 that they intended to breed 10 percent
more sows for fall litters than in 1953. If these fall plans are realized, the two 1954 pig crops would total about 91 million pigs. This
compares with the 82 million in 1953, and with a 93 million average for
1949-53.

        Production of early spring pigs this year was increased more than
late spring pigs. Twenty-one percent more sows farrowed in December to
March this season than last, whereas the increase in farrowings in April
and May was less than 1 percent. According to a quarterly pig crop report from 6 Corn Belt States, most of the increase in the fall pig crop
will be in summer-farrowed pigs.

        Hog slaughter was approaching last year's level by late June. As
marketings of early-farrowed spring pigs increase in July the slaughter
rate will climb above that of last year. It will stay above throughout
the fall months. Moreover, since more pigs will be produced this fall
than last, the rate of slaughter will continue higher the first part of
next year than in the like period of 1954.

        Prices of hogs in June were down from their April peak and below
prices in June last year. Prices of the heavy weights were reduced most
as late supplies of heavy barrows coincided with early marketings of sows.
Hog prices likely will be somewhat variable in the next few months and
will trend seasonally downward during the fall. The total seasonal reduction by the end of the year will be greater than average. Nevertheless,
pork supplies this fall will not be excessive as compared with recent
years and prices received by producers of hogs likely will remain rela-
tively favorable, with the hog-corn price ratio still somewhat above its
longtime average.

Slaughter of cattle in the first half of 1954 averaged about 10 percent above the corresponding period of 1953. It included more cows and heifers and about the same number of steers as last year. Total slaughter in the second half is expected to be roughly the same as in the like period last year. Slaughter of calves will likely continue above the 1953 volume. Combined cattle-and-calf slaughter for 1954 will nearly equal the number produced (less deaths), and will allow at most only a small increase in the number of cattle and calves on farms next January 1.

Total output of beef in 1954 will moderately exceed that in 1953, and consumption per person will not differ much from last year's record 77 pounds.

A larger movement of cattle into feedlots from December to May makes certain another large supply of fed cattle this summer and fall. Fed cattle prices, while remaining above 1953's low point, are not likely to increase at mid-summer as they did last year and will probably average somewhat lower this fall than last. Prices of grass cattle will probably make an approximately normal seasonal decline and may average not greatly different from last year.

Slightly more sheep and lambs were slaughtered in January to June this year than last. Although slaughter the rest of the year is expected to average a little less than last year, the year's total may be large enough to indicate a reduction in sheep inventories next January.

REVIEW AND OUTLOOK

Spring Pig Crop Up 13 Percent

Thirteen percent more pigs were saved in the spring pig crop this year than last. The number of sows farrowing was up 11 percent and a new high record of 6.9 pigs were saved per litter. (Table 1.)

This was the first increase in hog production since 1951. Discouraged by previous low prices and uncertain as to prices in the future, producers had cut back their production in 1952 and 1953. But higher prices for hogs in 1953 brought the production increase in 1954.

Almost all of the increase this spring was in early pigs. Farrowings in December to March were 21 percent greater this year than last, while farrowings in April and May were up less than 1 percent. (Table 2.) In recent years, producers have shifted more and more toward early farrowed pigs, aiming at the higher priced markets at mid-summer.

The record size of litter this spring is especially impressive in view of the large number of sows farrowing in winter and early spring months, when death losses of new-born pigs usually are highest. Favorable farrowing weather, further specialization in hog production, and favorable hog prices which encouraged better care contributed to the increase in size of litters this year.

Table 1 .- Number of sows farrowing, pigs saved and pigs saved per litter, spring
and fall pig crops, United States, by regions, 1948 to date

SPRING PIG CROP

Year	North Atlantic	North Central		South Atlantic	South Central	Western	United States
		East	West				
	Thousands	Thousands	Thousands	Thousands	Thousands	Thousands	Thousands
Sows farrowing							
1948	153	2,111	3,718	608	987	256	7,833
1949	165	2,394	4,319	633	1,053	256	8,820
1950	145	2,554	4,568	631	1,048	228	9,174
1951	153	2,625	4,855	683	1,026	249	9,591
1952	157	2,442	4,041	721	904	215	8,480
1953	136	2,219	3,600	597	603	145	7,300
1954 1/	127	2,449	4,042	626	716	168	8,128
Pigs saved							
1948	1,010	14,052	24,062	3,714	6,030	1,600	50,468
1949	1,107	15,909	27,835	3,909	6,570	1,639	56,969
1950	920	16,177	28,905	3,971	6,534	1,428	57,935
1951	1,016	17,238	31,463	4,273	6,430	1,587	62,007
1952	1,072	16,421	26,994	4,601	5,846	1,336	56,270
1953	942	15,313	24,635	3,910	3,947	956	49,703
1954 1/	870	17,083	28,014	4,187	4,798	1,114	56,066
Pigs saved per litter	Number	Number	Number	Number	Number	Number	Number
1948	6.58	6.65	6.47	6.11	6.11	6.26	6.44
1949	6.73	6.65	6.44	6.17	6.24	6.39	6.46
1950	6.36	6.33	6.33	6.29	6.23	6.26	6.31
1951	6.63	6.57	6.48	6.26	6.27	6.38	6.47
1952	6.83	6.72	6.68	6.38	6.47	6.23	6.64
1953	6.92	6.90	6.84	6.55	6.55	6.59	6.81
1954 1/	6.87	6.98	6.93	6.69	6.70	6.61	6.90

FALL PIG CROP

Year	North Atlantic	North Central		South Atlantic	South Central	Western	United States
		East	West				
Sows farrowing	Thousands	Thousands	Thousands	Thousands	Thousands	Thousands	Thousands
1948	126	1,609	1,690	551	904	190	5,070
1949	123	1,800	1,941	565	951	188	5,568
1950	119	1,970	2,183	561	924	166	5,923
1951	126	1,991	2,237	610	879	189	6,032
1952	118	1,781	1,976	555	684	143	5,257
1953	96	1,672	1,842	463	574	115	4,762
1954 2/	97	1,881	1,998	504	643	137	5,260
Pigs saved							
1948	865	10,917	11,184	3,452	5,717	1,223	33,358
1949	831	11,925	12,694	3,531	6,059	1,235	36,275
1950	815	13,289	14,674	3,552	5,998	1,076	39,404
1951	872	13,346	14,690	3,968	5,704	1,224	39,804
1952	818	11,972	13,252	3,559	4,420	940	34,961
1953	661	11,290	12,310	3,076	3,788	757	31,882
1954							2/35,000
Pigs saved per litter	Number	Number	Number	Number	Number	Number	Number
1948	6.88	6.78	6.62	6.27	6.32	6.43	6.58
1949	6.77	6.62	6.54	6.25	6.37	6.55	6.52
1950	6.83	6.74	6.72	6.33	6.49	6.50	6.65
1951	6.92	6.70	6.57	6.51	6.49	6.47	6.60
1952	6.97	6.72	6.71	6.41	6.46	6.56	6.65
1953	6.91	6.75	6.68	6.65	6.60	6.58	6.70
1954							2/6.70

1/ Preliminary.
2/ Number indicated to farrow from breeding intentions as of June 1, 1954. Average number of pigs per
litter with allowance for trend used to calculate indicated number of pigs saved.

Table 2.- Number of sows farrowing and percentage distribution by
months, spring season, United States, 1948-54

Year	Dec. 1/	Jan.	Feb.	Mar.	Apr.	May	Total
	Thous.	Thous.	Thous.	Thous.	Thous.	Thous.	Thous.
1948	254	350	746	2,122	2,838	1,523	7,833
1949	283	441	958	2,567	3,026	1,545	8,820
1950	249	416	1,089	2,803	3,084	1,533	9,174
1951	288	491	1,237	2,752	3,103	1,720	9,591
1952	267	480	1,198	2,385	2,586	1,564	8,480
1953	220	441	1,050	2,108	2,221	1,260	7,300
1954	274	515	1,410	2,428	2,213	1,288	8,128
	Percentage of total sows farrowing						
	Percent	Percent	Percent	Percent	Percent	Percent	Percent
1948	3.2	4.5	9.5	27.1	36.2	19.5	100.0
1949	3.2	5.0	10.9	29.1	34.3	17.5	100.0
1950	2.7	4.5	11.9	30.6	33.6	16.7	100.0
1951	3.0	5.1	12.9	28.7	32.4	17.9	100.0
1952	3.2	5.7	14.1	28.1	30.5	18.4	100.0
1953	3.0	6.0	14.4	28.9	30.4	17.3	100.0
1954	3.4	6.3	17.4	29.9	27.2	15.8	100.0

1/ December of preceding year.

All regions except the North Atlantic shared in the spring expansion in the pig crop.

Fall Crop Indicated
10 Percent Larger

Farmers reported as of June 1 their intentions to farrow 10 percent more sows this fall than last. At an average size of litter adjusted for trend the number of pigs also would be 10 percent greater. All regions showed probable increases in fall farrowings.

Most of the increase in the fall pig crop will be of summer-farrowed pigs. In 6 Corn Belt States producers intend to step up their June-August farrowings by 20 percent, but September-November farrowings by only 2 percent, according to a quarterly pig crop report issued June 22 through the State-Federal Crop Reporting Service in the 6 States. This shift toward summer pigs, which also has been taking place for several years, is comparable to that toward winter pigs in the spring pig crop. The two changes tend to smooth out the seasonality in farrowings. The traditional bunching of farrowings in March-April and August-September is being reduced. Correspondingly, less of the total marketings are now crowded into late fall and mid-spring months. (For a discussion of these trends see the Livestock and Meat Situation for May 7, 1954, pp. 12-13.)

If farmers' intentions for fall pigs are realized the 1954 combined pig crops--spring and fall--will be 91 million pigs. This is 9.5 million above 1953, but 10.7 million below 1951, and a little below the average of 93 million pigs the last 5 years.

Hog Slaughter in June Moderately Below
Last Year, Prices Also Lower

Hog slaughter in January of this year was 25 percent below a year earlier. Since January the rate of slaughter has been closer to last year's level, and in May and June averaged only about 6 to 7 percent less than a year before. This was a high rate of slaughter for those months in view of the sharply fewer pigs born in September and October last fall. Slaughter was high because many barrows and gilts were kept for late marketing at heavy weights, and because early marketings of sows were greater this year than last. Delayed marketing of heavy hogs is shown by the 12 pounds heavier average weights of barrows and gilts at central markets in May and June this year. Receipts of sows in the two months were nearly 20 percent larger than at the same time last year. More sows were marketed early because more farrowed early and thus were ready for sale in the first part of the summer marketing season.

Prices of hogs generally declined after reaching a high in April. They recovered somewhat in late June but were still several dollars per 100 pounds below the high mark in late April, and were a little below prices in June 1953.

Prices of heavy hogs declined most. Hogs of 180-200 pounds declined $3.36 per 100 pounds over the two months but 240-270 pound barrows and gilts were off $4.25 and prices of sows were down $5.90 (Chicago prices). The sharper reductions for heavy hogs resulted in part from larger supplies of those weights, but also reflected packers' anticipations of a lower price trend for lard and other fat pork products, as well as pork, as hog slaughter increases. Lard prices, after having been depressed for several years, advanced materially in the last year or two of reduced supplies. They will likely average lower in the next year or two.

As increasing numbers of winter-farrowed pigs are marketed in coming weeks, slaughter of hogs will rise above last year. Slaughter will continue above in months ahead.

The number of hogs slaughtered in the entire fall season will be greater than that in 1953, about in line with the 13 percent rise in the spring pig crop. Much of the increase will be in early months of the fall season. Last year, hog slaughter turned upward in August, advanced sharply in mid-September, and hit its peak in November, a month before it usually does. Because so many pigs were farrowed in winter months this year the upturn in slaughter will come even sooner this summer. The weekly slaughter rate will probably be variable, and prices are likely to fluctuate considerably. Each increase in prices will probably be followed by temporarily large marketings of light-weight hogs. However, as prices started downward early, the proportion of hogs marketed young and light will probably be no greater than last year. Marketings may be maintained well in late fall, since quite a few producers having pigs born in March to May may be inclined to hold their hogs past November, which was the

month of largest slaughter and lowest prices in 1953. On the whole, the
prospects are for (1) larger late summer marketings than last year; (2)
marketing of a smaller percentage of the total spring crop in the 10 weeks
from late September through November; and (3) a general high marketing
rate from October to December, instead of a November peak such as last
year.

Another reason for expecting marketings to be spread out over a
longer period this year than last is the tendency for the larger producers
who make most of the shift to early pigs also to feed their hogs fastest
for early marketings. Small producers, who generally have later farrowings, feed for slower gain. Thus early pigs will be marketed earlier than
usual, and late pigs perhaps later than usual, lengthening the marketing
season. Data on these shifts by producers were recently reported from an
Iowa-Illinois survey.

Since the fall pig crop of 1954, like the spring crop, will be substantially above last year's, the higher level of hog slaughter will continue through at least the first half of 1955. Slaughter later in 1955
will be governed by the size of the 1955 spring pig crop. Although prospects for that crop are not yet clear, there is a strong likelihood that
it will be increased.

Hog slaughter this fall and winter, though substantially above last
year's, will not be excessive. Supplies of pork per person will be no
greater than average.

Price trends for any class of livestock are usually erratic in a
period of readjustment. This will probably prove to be the case for hogs
this year. Hog prices may vary considerably this summer, and they will
trace a general seasonal decline until late fall. The overall decline
will be greater than in an average year and prices will be lower than in
the same period last year. However, prices are expected to remain favorable to producers. The hog-corn price ratio likely will stay somewhat
above its longtime average.

Price differences between light and heavy hogs will be narrowed this
summer as marketings of lighter hogs increase and heavy hogs decline.
Later in the fall, however, discounts for heavy hogs will reappear. It is
unlikely that price relationships will favor feeding to as heavy weight
as they did last fall and winter.

Cattle Slaughter 10 Percent
Above Last Year in First Half

About 10 percent more cattle were slaughtered in the first half of
1954 than in the first half of 1953. The slaughter this year was a new
high record for this period.

The increase was in cows and heifers slaughtered. Cow slaughter
under Federal inspection from January through May was up 34 percent from
1953, and heifer slaughter was up 29 percent. (June data are not yet avail
able.)

Steer slaughter, which was large in 1953, recorded no further increa
for the first half of 1954. The January-May total was 1 percent below that
of last year. (Table 3.)

Table 3.- Number of cattle slaughtered under Federal inspection, by class, 1954 compared with 1953.

Month	Steers		Heifers		Cows		Calves	
	1954	1953	1954	1953	1954	1953	1954	1953
	1,000 head	1,000 head	1,000 head	1,000 head	1,000 head	1,000 head	1,000 head	1,000 head
January	774	709	250	179	487	390	546	453
February	673	692	201	165	400	287	518	422
March	825	802	212	153	440	308	660	535
April	806	869	173	152	402	304	698	541
May	815	854	155	122	429	319	561	504
June		890		135		371		586
July		849		165		431		616
August		774		178		492		602
September		781		189		618		687
October		752		219		755		776
November		693		183		690		658
December		779		208		625		634
Year 1/		9,445		2,049		5,591		7,013

1/ Computed from unrounded numbers.

Compiled from Market News, Livestock Division

Included in the number of steers slaughtered were somewhat fewer fed steers this year than last. Receipts of slaughter steers at 3 mid-West markets in January-May were 7 percent less than in the same 1953 period. Although 9 percent fewer cattle were on feed this January than in January 1953, more were placed on feed each month from January through May and movements out of feedlots have been rather early and rapid. Lighter weights for each grade indicate that many cattle were sold quickly after a shorter feeding period. The result has been a marketing rate a little higher in relation to inventories this year than last.

Cattle Slaughter May Not Exceed
Last Year in Second Half

Speeded by drought, cattle slaughter increased more than usual during the fall of 1953. There are some indications that slaughter will not rise so much this year. It may not average any larger in the second half of this year than last.

Roughly as many fed cattle will be marketed in the second half of this year as last. Although fewer cattle apparently moved into feedlots in June this year than last, the larger earlier placements probably lifted the level of feeding this summer to around that of last summer. (An estimate of the number on feed July 1 will be released July 14.)

Fewer grass steers are expected to be marketed in the second half of 1954 than in 1953. Fewer are available; the total inventory of steers on January 1 was down 11 percent from last year, and the inventory of beef calves was practically unchanged. Also, from the smaller supply somewhat more will likely go into feedlots instead of directly to slaughter.

On the other hand, slaughter of cows and heifers will continue larger in most months this fall than last, although by a much smaller percentage than in the first 6 months.

Weather and feed conditions will have much to do with the actual slaughter rate this fall. The severe drought in the Southern Plains was broken by spring rains. If favorable weather continues, slaughter of cows and of steers, heifers and calves off grass will be somewhat smaller than it would be under pressure of dry range and short feed supplies.

Calf Slaughter Above 1953

About 15 percent more calves were slaughtered in the first 6 months this year than last. Calf slaughter will likely be moderately larger this fall than last.

Prospective slaughter rates are of interest not only as they affect concurrent meat output and livestock prices but also in their relation to livestock inventories and production in the future. If from July to December, 2 to 5 percent more calves and the same number of cattle are slaughtered as in the same period last year, combined slaughter of cattle and calves for 1954 would be around 39 million. A reasonable forecast of the calf crop and of death losses would indicate a net increase a little greater than 39 million. The number of cattle on farms next January may, therefore, be expected to increase slightly. If slaughter is much above the prospective rate, cattle inventories will be held about unchanged or reduced next January. But regardless of whether the inventory of cattle and calves finally shows a small increase or a small decrease this year, it will remain very large. In either case the outlook will be for a substantial annual supply of beef in the next year or longer.

Cattle Prices Lower

Prices of all grades and classes of cattle have declined from early spring highs. To some degree these were seasonal price changes, though not of exactly normal pattern. The declines for fed cattle in particular were delayed, beginning in April instead of earlier in the year. Since prices for lower grade slaughter steers did not turn down until mid-June, the seasonal narrowing of the price spread between higher and lower grades, which usually comes at mid-spring, was a little later this year.

Choice steers at Chicago averaged $23.50 to $24.00 per 100 pounds in late June, $1.00 less than in April and $2.00 above prices in June last year. Prices of this grade usually turn upward in late summer; last year they advanced about $4. Prices probably will not make a comparable increase this year and in late summer will likely be below prices a year

earlier. The large supply of fed cattle to be.marketed will tend to
limit prices. Even though pork is not highly competitive with beef,
the larger supply of pork will have some influence on prices of cattle.
Nevertheless, the most important factor to affect fed cattle prices this
summer will be the rate of marketing. Fed cattle have moved into slaughter in an orderly manner, with no great gluts at any time. This has
contributed to the comparative stability of prices. If marketings continue orderly, with little bunching, stability and moderate strength in
prices will continue.

Seasonal Declines in Grass Cattle Prices

Prices of stocker and feeder cattle had turned seasonally downward
by late June but were several dollars higher than in the same weeks of
last year, when drought forced prices to a temporary low. A general seasonal decline is in view this summer and fall. But the seasonal downtrend
may be approximately normal, in contrast with declines which were late in 1952
and early in 1953. Prices of all grass cattle may average roughly the
same as last year. Like last year, there may be considerable price var-
iation among kinds of cattle and among regions. Buyers of both feeder
and slaughter cattle may show a marked preference for the higher grades
of grass cattle, although the price spread between grades may not be
quite as wide as it was last year. Last fall, prices of Common feeder
steers were farther below Choice feeders (in percent) than in any other
year of record. Some areas where cattle production has increased most
rapidly still lack a strong market demand for their grass cattle. Prices
in these areas will again be below the general average.

January-June Sheep and Lamb
Slaughter Slightly Exceeds Last Year

About 2 percent more sheep and lambs were slaughtered in January-
June this year than last. The larger number of early spring lambs produced this year and fast development of these lambs in most areas contributed to the fairly high slaughter.

The year's total lamb crop is expected to be smaller than the 1953
crop and sheep and lamb slaughter in the second half of 1954 will probably
be smaller than last year. However, unless slaughter is reduced considerably, the year's total will be big enough to indicate a further decrease
in sheep inventories next January 1. The number of sheep and lambs on
farms, after increasing from a 1950 low, was reduced in each of the last
2 years.

Price movements for lambs have been much different this year than
last. In 1953, prices of spring lambs opened at higher levels than old-
crop fed lambs. Prices held up well through July, then declined rapidly.
This year, spring lambs at the beginning of the season sold for no more
than had previously been received for fed lambs, and spring lamb prices
declined in June.

In view of the prospects for a smaller supply of lambs this fall
than last, for reasonably stable prices for fed cattle and for about normal price trends for grass cattle, prices of lambs may be maintained fairly
close to their lower level of June. Their further seasonal decline may be
no greater than usual.

Total Meat Supply in Second Half
    to Exceed 1953

    With more pork, approximately the same quantity of beef, and slightly
less lamb and mutton to be produced in the second half of 1954 than of 1953,
the total output of red meat will be moderately larger. In the first half
the total output was not much different from the previous year.

    Consumption of beef per person in 1954 will be about the same as
last year's 77 pounds. Because of reductions in the first half, 1954 pork
consumption will fall slightly short of the 63 pounds of last year.

NEW OR REVISED SERIES

Edible Offals

    Data on meat production do not include the quantities of liver,
heart, head meat and other edible offals that are produced each year.
Table 4 brings forward estimates of production and distribution of these
products. An explanation of the nature and sources of the data may be
found in this Situation for May 1949.

    Revisions in prices received by farmers for meat animals in 1953
and related data are contained in table 5.

LIVESTOCK PRODUCTS AS A SOURCE OF FARMERS' INCOME

    Farmers as a group now receive more than half their cash income
from livestock and livestock products--and for the last 8 years sales of
meat animals have produced over half the livestock total. Preliminary
data for 1953 show that 55 percent of the farmer's cash receipts (cash
receipts from farm marketings and government payments to farmers) came
from the sale of livestock and livestock products and 28.5 percent was
from meat animals. Cattle and calves made up 15.7, hogs 11.8, and sheep
and lambs 1.0 percent of the total. Wool, classed separately from sheep
and lambs, added 0.4 percent of the total.(Table 6.)

    Income from all livestock has not only increased greatly the past 40
years but has made up an increasingly larger part of the total farm income.
In 1910-14, 49.6 percent of the farm receipts came from livestock, compared
with the 55.0 percent in 1953. This increase results from marketing more
and more of the feed crops as livestock or livestock products, and from
declines in the proportion of receipts from cotton and from wheat. During
the 1920's receipts from cotton (lint and seed) were about equal to those
from cattle and calves; in 1953, they were about 37 percent less than the
receipts from cattle and calves. Changes in dietary habits are reflected
in the declining proportion of receipts from wheat and other food grains.

Continued page 15

Table 4. - Edible offals: Supply and distribution, United States, 1934 to date.

Year	Supply Total production 1/ Mil. lb.	Supply Beginning commercial stocks 2/ Mil. lb.	Supply Imports Mil. lb.	Supply Total supply Mil. lb.	Distribution Ending commercial stocks 2/ Mil. lb.	Distribution Commercial exports and shipments 3/ Mil. lb.	Distribution Domestic disappearance Military Mil. lb.	Distribution Domestic disappearance Civilian Mil. lb.	Distribution Domestic disappearance Civilian per capita 4/ Lb.
1934	1,298	65	5/	1,363	126	28	---	1,209	9.4
1935	904	126	1	1,121	74	17	---	1,030	8.0
1936	1,152	74	5/	1,226	132	18	---	1,076	8.3
1937	1,083	132	1	1,216	67	14	---	1,135	8.7
1938	1,130	67	5/	1,197	72	19	---	1,106	8.4
1939	1,200	72	1	1,273	95	19	---	1,159	8.7
1940	1,303	95	2	1,400	102	11	---	1,287	9.6
1941	1,338	102	4	1,444	105	8	---	1,331	10.0
1942	1,498	105	2	1,605	86	11	5/	1,508	11.3
1943	1,669	86	5/	1,755	137	22	2	1,594	12.2
1944	1,740	97 6/	5/	1,837	37	68	2	1,730	13.3
1945	1,637	37	5/	1,674	41	3	3	1,627	12.4
1946	1,579	41	5/	1,620	56	1	5/	1,563	11.1
1947	1,615	56	5/	1,671	71	9	5/	1,591	11.0
1948	1,472	71	5	1,548	58	1	5/	1,489	10.1
1949	1,495	58	10	1,563	62	2	5/	1,499	10.0
1950	1,519	52	9	1,590	59	3	5/	1,528	10.0
1951	1,502	59	8	1,569	64	6	5/	1,499	9.8
1952	1,580	64	8	1,652	69	7/4	5/	1,579	10.2
1953	1,712	69	7	1,788	59	7/25	5/	1,704	10.8

1/ Production of offals as percentage of dressed weight of meat production, including farm: Beef 6.7, veal 10.7, lamb and mutton 5.1, pork excluding lard 6.7. 2/ Trimmings included prior to July 1, 1944; excluded beginning that date. 3/ Exports only beginning 1951, as shipment data not reported. 4/ Calculated from number of persons eating out of civilian supplies July 1 adjusted for underenumeration. 5/ Less than 500,000 pounds. 6/ Adjusted by 40 million pounds as estimat allowance for trimmings, which were reported in stocks prior to July 1, 1944. 7/ Bureau of Census reports classification of "other meats except canned including edible animal organs)" which includes sausage ingredients. 4 million pounds were deducted as an estimated quantity of sausage ingredients in 1953.

Table 5 .- Price per 100 pounds received by farmers for meat animals by classes, index numbers of prices received for meat animals, and hog-corn price ratio, United States, by months 1953-54

Commodity and year	Jan.	Feb.	Mar.	Apr.	May	June	July	Aug.	Sept.	Oct.	Nov.	Dec.	Weighted average
	Dol.	Dol.	Dol.	Dol.	Dol.	Dol.	Dol.	Dol.	Dol.	Dol.	Dol.	Dol.	Dol.
Beef cattle													
1953	19.10	18.50	17.70	17.30	17.50	16.00	17.10	16.10	15.60	14.60	14.50	14.80	16.30
1954	16.00	16.20	16.60	17.10	17.60	16.90							
Veal calves													
1953	22.10	22.10	2.10	19.30	19.40	16.50	16.80	16.10	14.80	13.80	14.50	15.60	16.80
1954	17.80	18.10	17.90	18.10	18.40	17.50							
Hogs													
1953	17.90	19.30	20.20	21.00	23.10	22.80	23.70	23.30	23.90	21.30	20.30	23.00	21.40
1954	24.60	25.30	24.70	26.60	25.70	21.70							
Sheep													
1953	7.95	8.24	8.43	8.29	7.89	6.39	6.08	6.10	5.81	5.72	5.98	6.33	6.63
1954	7.11	7.39	8.02	7.56	7.01	6.66							
Lambs													
1953	20.40	20.50	20.40	20.80	22.10	21.80	21.60	20.00	17.60	16.6	17.10	17.30	19.30
1954	18.60	19.10	20.90	21.80	21.80	20.30							
Index numbers of prices received for meat animals, Jan. 1910-Dec. 1914 = 100													
	Pct.	Pct.	Pct.	Pct.	Pct.	Pct.	Pct.	Pct.	Pct.	Pct.	Pct.	Pct.	Pct.
1953	303	305	301	299	317	300	319	305	299	273	267	285	2/298
1954	309	315	316	333	331	299							
Hog-Corn Ratio United States 1/													
	Pct.	Pct.	Pct.	Pct.	Pct.	Pct.	Pct.	Pct.	Pct.	Pct.	Pct.	Pct.	Pct.
1953	12.1	13.5	13.8	14.4	15.5	15.6	16.1	15.7	15.9	15.9	15.3	16.3	2/15.0
1954	17.3	17.7	17.2	18.3	17.5	14.6							
Chicago													
1953	11.4	12.7	13.3	14.2	15.2	16.2	16.4	15.2	14.9	14.7	14.4	15.5	2/14.5
1954	16.2	16.7	16.7	17.5	16.4								

1/ United States, based on prices received by farmers for all hogs.   2/ Unweighted average.

Revises and brings to date table A-14 of this Situation released March 5, 1954.

Table 6.- Percentage of cash farm receipts by source, selected years.

Year	Livestock and livestock products					Crops	Government payments	Total
	Meat animals	Dairy products	Eggs and poultry	Other	Total			
	Percent	Percent	Percent	Percent	Percent	Percent	Percent	Percent
Average: 1910-14	28.4	10.6	8.1	2.5	49.6	50.4	0	100.0
1919	27.8	10.4	7.6	1.7	47.5	52.5	0	100.0
1929	26.7	16.3	10.5	1.2	54.7	45.3	0	100.0
1939	26.5	15.7	9.0	1.5	52.7	38.4	8.9	100.0
1949	29.6	13.3	11.1	.6	54.6	44.7	.7	100.0
1953	28.5	13.7	12.1	.7	55.0	44.3	.7	100.0

Meat animals accounted for about the same percentage of total cash receipts last year as in 1910-14. Dairy and poultry products were a larger part than in 1910-14. Dairy products gained in relative importance in the early 1920's but have lost some ground since. The advance in position for poultry products has been more gradual and continuous.

From 1920 to 1944, dairy products were a source of more income than were cattle and calves. Since 1945, cattle and calves have been the largest single source of income. In 1953 receipts for cattle were one-third greater than those from hogs and one-seventh greater than from dairy products. However, receipts from the sale of cattle and calves include marketings of cattle and calves born of dairy cows. If receipts from dairy stock sold for beef and from veal calves were added to dairy receipts and subtracted from cattle and calves, the total from dairying would be the largest source of cash receipts.

The income received from sales of livestock and livestock products represents the value of feeds fed as well as the value of all other items in production. They include values of feeder and breeding stock bought by farmers after shipment from other States. Comparisons based on sales thus give livestock a higher place than do those based on the value of (net) production. On the basis of the value of production or output, in which the value of feeds is credited to the feed crops and deducted from the value of livestock, livestock amounted to 25 percent of the value of total farm output.

Selected Price Statistics for Meat Animals 1/

Item	Unit	1953 Year total or average	Apr.	May	1954 Apr.	May	June
Cattle and calves							
Beef steers, slaughter	:Dollars per:						
Chicago, Prime	:100 pounds	26.56	23.58	23.51	27.96	26.67	
Choice	do.	24.14	21.99	22.36	24.83	24.25	
Good	do.	21.56	20.37	20.95	21.77	21.79	
Commercial	do.	18.74	18.68	19.07	18.78	18.99	
Utility	do.	15.77	16.52	17.06	15.88	16.42	
All grades	do.	23.62	21.50	21.83	23.77	23.54	
Omaha, all grades	do.	21.91	20.88	20.97	22.23	22.46	
Sioux City, all grades	do.	22.10	20.11	20.94	22.47	22.25	
Cows, Chicago							
Commercial	do.	13.92	15.34	15.12	14.81	15.18	
Utility	do.	12.41	14.11	13.57	12.85	13.50	
Canner and Cutter	do.	10.67	12.39	11.44	10.64	11.52	
Vealers, Choice and Prime, Chicago	do.	25.04	26.28	26.25	24.80	23.80	
Stocker and feeder steers, Kansas City 2/	do.	17.35	19.91	19.80	20.62	20.44	
Price received by farmers							
Beef cattle	do.	16.30	17.30	17.50	17.10	17.60	16.90
Veal calves	do.	16.80	19.30	19.40	18.10	18.40	17.50
Hogs							
Barrows and gilts							
Chicago							
160-180 pounds	do.	21.82	21.06	23.23	26.46	25.78	
180-200 pounds	do.	22.86	22.18	24.46	27.67	27.07	
200-220 pounds	do.	22.99	22.32	24.58	27.84	27.15	
220-240 pounds	do.	22.94	22.32	24.58	27.78	25.80	
240-270 pounds	do.	22.75	22.38	24.48	27.47	25.99	
270-300 pounds	do.	22.26	21.97	24.15	27.09	25.08	
All weights	do.	22.03	22.29	24.32	27.30	26.05	24.02
Eight markets 3/	do.	21.99	22.11	24.01	27.30	26.09	
Sows, Chicago	do.	20.56	20.24	21.68	24.17	21.23	18.52
Price received by farmers	do.	21.40	21.00	23.10	26.60	25.70	21.70
Hog-corn price ratio 4/							
Chicago, barrows and gilts	do.	14.5	14.2	15.2	17.5	16.4	14.9
Price received by farmers, all hogs	do.	15.0	14.4	15.5	18.3	17.5	14.6
Sheep and lambs							
Sheep							
Slaughter ewes, Good and Choice, Chicago	do.	7.14	9.72	6.60	8.12	5.88	
Price received by farmers	do.	6.63	8.29	7.89	7.56	7.01	6.66
Lambs							
Slaughter, Choice and Prime Chicago	do.	22.94	24.12	25.85	25.42	23.00	
Feeding, Good and Choice, Omaha	do.	18.36	----	----	22.31	----	
Price received by farmers	do.	19.30	20.80	22.10	21.80	21.80	20.30
All meat animals							
Index number price received by farmers							
(1910-14=100)		298	299	317	333	331	299
Meat							
Wholesale, Chicago	:Dollars per:						
Steer beef carcass, Choice, 500-600 pounds	:100 pounds	39.78	36.46	37.36	39.45	40.01	
Lamb carcass, Choice, 40-50 pounds	do.	44.68	45.36	49.48	48.75	48.35	
Composite hog products,							
Including lard	Dollars						
72.84 pounds fresh	do.	23.85	23.03	24.91	28.56	27.97	
Average per 100 pounds	do.	32.74	31.62	34.20	39.21	38.40	
71.19 pounds fresh and cured	do.	27.53	26.49	28.39	31.93	31.90	
Average per 100 pounds	do.	38.67	37.21	39.88	44.85	44.81	
Excluding lard							
56.19 pounds fresh and cured	do.	25.11	24.39	26.23	28.32	28.53	
Average per 100 pounds	do.	44.69	43.41	46.68	50.40	50.77	
Retail, United States average	Cents						
Beef, Choice grade	per pound	69.6	66.8	66.0	67.3	68.3	
Pork, excluding lard	do.	54.1	51.2	54.9	58.3	58.7	
Index number meat prices (BLS)							
Wholesale (1947-49 = 100)		92.1	88.2	92.7	93.9	99.1	

1/ Annual data for most series published in Statistical Appendix to this Situation, released March 5, 1954.
2/ Average all weights and grades.
3/ Chicago, St. Louis N. S. Y., Kansas City, Omaha, Sioux City, S. St. Joseph, S. St. Paul, and Indianapolis.
4/ Number bushels of corn equivalent in value to 100 pounds of live hogs.

Selected marketing, slaughter and stocks statistics for meat animals and meats 1/

Item	Unit	1953 Year total or average	1953 Apr.	1953 May	1954 Apr.	1954 May	June
Meat animal marketings							
Index number (1935-39=100)		160	152	141	145	145	
Stocker and feeder shipments to 9 Corn Belt States	1,000						
Cattle and calves	head	3,532	161	160	217	181	
Sheep and lambs	do.	2,907	99	131	202	147	
Slaughter under Federal inspection							
Number slaughtered							
Cattle	do.	17,629	1,371	1,345	1,417	1,439	
Calves	do.	7,013	541	504	698	561	
Sheep and lambs	do.	14,283	1,100	1,015	1,096	1,045	
Hogs	do.	53,813	4,325	3,643	3,853	3,380	
Percentage sows	Percent	9.9	6.0	12.3	8.2	17.4	
Average live weight per head							
Cattle	Pounds	970	988	984	970	960	
Calves	do.	227	197	229	196	218	
Sheep and lambs	do.	95	100	96	99	96	
Hogs	do.	238	233	244	246	261	
Average production							
Beef, per head	do.	533	560	558	541	538	
Veal, per head	do.	126	112	129	110	121	
Lamb and mutton, per head	do.	45	48	46	48	46	
Pork, per head 2/	do.	136	132	138	142	150	
Pork, per 100 pounds live weight 2/	do.	57	57	57	58	58	
Lard, per head	do.	34	34	35	34	37	
Lard, per 100 pounds live weight	do.	14	14	14	14	14	
Total production	Million						
Beef	pounds	9,368	766	748	763	770	
Veal	do.	882	60	65	66	68	
Lamb and mutton	do.	644	52	47	52	48	
Pork 2/	do.	7,293	570	502	548	505	
Lard	do.	1,812	146	128	131	125	
Total commercial slaughter 3/							
Number slaughtered	1,000						
Cattle	head	23,605	1,847	1,804	1,919	1,964	
Calves	do.	11,668	915	848	992	948	
Sheep and lambs	do.	15,967	1,227	1,136	1,235	1,177	
Hogs	do.	66,913	5,450	4,548	4,724	4,205	
Total production	Million						
Beef	pounds	12,055	989	961	990	1,009	
Veal	do.	1,451	102	107	111	115	
Lamb and mutton	do.	715	58	52	58	54	
Pork 2/	do.	8,971	714	619	661	616	
Lard	do.	2,122	174	150	153	145	
Cold storage stocks first of month							
Beef	do.	----	235	218	173	147	127
Veal	do.	----	21	17	14	13	11
Lamb and mutton	do.	----	20	17	9	9	8
Pork	do.	----	569	538	418	421	392
Total meat and meat products 4/	do.	----	990	929	732	706	657

1/ Annual data for most series published in Statistical Appendix to this Situation, released March 5, 1954
2/ Excludes lard.
3/ Federally inspected, and other wholesale and retail.
4/ Includes stocks of sausage and sausage room products, canned meats and canned meat products, and edible offals, in addition to the four meats listed.

Lightning Source UK Ltd.
Milton Keynes UK
UKHW011153051118
331792UK00005B/139/P